Chained Dog Dreams

poems by

Carol D. Guerrero-Murphy

Finishing Line Press
Georgetown, Kentucky

Chained Dog Dreams

ACKNOWLEDGMENTS

"My Galapagos." *Comstock Review*. New York. Fall 2013.

"The Camel and the Mastodon Reply." *Ibid.*

"To Pray at the Altar of This Horse." *Even Cowboys Carry Cell Phones; Manifest West
Anthology, Western State University*. Teresa Mildbrodt., ed. Colorado University Press.
September 2013.

"'Horse Says" published as "Lucky Says." *Ibid.*

"Look at Us Becoming Older with Grace." *Pilgrimage*. Vol. 35.3 Maria Meléndez, editor.
Pueblo, CO. December 2011.

"November Pasture Song, under the name 'Love Song for Lucky,'" in *Tales from the Hidden
Lake*. Anthology. First prize poetry. Southern Peaks Library. Fall 2009.

"Time to See." *Telling it Real: 10 Years of Pilgrimage*. Anthology. Peter Anderson, Ed.
Spring 2010.

"Time to See." *Pilgrimage*. Peter Anderson, editor. vol. 34. Crestone, CO 2005.

Publisher: Leah Maines
Editor: Christen Kincaid
Cover Art: David Diaz Guerrero
Author Photo: Linda Relyea
Cover Design: Elizabeth Maines McCleavy

Printed in the USA on acid-free paper.
Order online: www.finishinglinepress.com
also available on amazon.com

Author inquiries and mail orders:
Finishing Line Press
P. O. Box 1626
Georgetown, Kentucky 40324
U. S. A.

Table of Contents

WOMAN DESCENDING A STAIR

THANKS

For My Family

And for Lucky the Mustang

STAR DATE UNKNOWN

Route 66 Summer 1958

We drove fast as rain over our blue highway.
The highway undressed far horizon button-by-button.
My father's mercy furrowed the road ahead with possibility.
My mother's wound baked in the front seat,
just a memory it was, but painful as parched earth.
The wound ploughed her skin with infection.
I sat in the back holding Frank's fishbowl
and thought about a silver lake, a cooling swim,
hot dogs, mildewed canvas tents. Frank's guppies sloshed
to the sound of the wheels praying.
A potato chip had wrecked itself on our motel's kitchen floor.
The final detail of a thousand wrecks from the night before.

May Pole Dance 1956

We wove a pattern of ribbons over and under,
skipped and wove but when I remember this I remember
my mother calling out the door after my father
words I cannot write, hate among them,
and I played The Blob oozing invisible under a bedspread,
creeping along the sidewalk,
able to swallow anything whole.

In the Sugar Pines 2001

They dropped their cones, hankies on the fornicating forest floor.
Yes, in the atlas of a meadow, drawn by burrowing groundhogs,
mad and happy fornication of which the sky has no inkling
is going on. And on. To stumble on the lace leaves
of those punctured plantains, the nasal voice of ravens,
not the caw but the trilling giggle of their courtship,
to breathe the sweet umbels of wild celery,
all of that which frightened might seem a salve
to seal disgust as childish as a child who won't won't won't
eat radishes.

Stone Memory, the Cherry Song 1964

Beneath a mint-cookie thin paver
a thick maggotish root with branching roots
feathers out in a compass rose.
The root is pressed into earth dark and smooth;
a miniscule spider squiggles across it.
Do not kill fear-rousing things solely
due to their micro-scale. Listen.
What are the root, the dark, the spider?
The root is named Spring of the Bay of Pigs,
Autumn of the Cuban Missile Crisis.
The dark pressed soil is the playground
I raced across to home from school
to say goodbye to my family before the sky
whitened to absence.

Abbreviated Autobiography of Mincing

Mine is a history of mincing
the beach's triangular, succulent ice plants,
the forest's black spruce buds sticky and tender,
crisp garlic bulbs stolen from the kitchen.
The lies I told about them.
Ice plant mucous pooled from the minced stems
I instructed my friends
will close gashes.
Spruce buds minced with pond water
smeared over the face repel all biting insects.
Garlic minced and spread on oil slick inlet clay
will change the tides. What didn't I know?

I ask Virginia Crowell of Turnagain by the Sea
Quality Homes in Anchorage, Alaska,
to forgive me for that difficult night
we tried to sleep in the woods behind our houses
when she cut her thumb and bled and bled
despite my cure and mosquitoes swarmed us both.
While we slapped, the summer sun sailed all night.
The waters rose. Did our stick and vine raft float away?

Broken Tooth Speaks

I come from a bucket of broken teeth
in a room full of ice and coal engaged
in war, quiet and sharp.
I am a chip off an ivory crown whose jewels have gone missing
sunk into slag river and ash pile.
My country, my animal is forgotten, extinct.
My mother sailed from there.
She gnawed wood to feed me.
Lashed to a pole she birthed me.
She told me this story, herself a broken tooth,
small, stained ochre, hungry
for fruit and clicking.
I eat the meat of her story, I eat the air
that whistles through me.
When I sleep I return to that bucket.
I dream we are clicking together,
dream of our dancing jaw.

The Camel and the Mastodon Vertebrae Reply

We write to reply to your constant queries
and your bizarre remarks about shivers when you hear our names,
your gossip and rumors about our whereabouts,
our demise, surmises about our companions.
We attempt to reply to the little girl
who you say lives within you
and may be the source of your irritating why why why why why.
We do not know the nature of our charms.
Undoubtedly once we knelt on the sedimentary floor of your valley
then lay all the way down, stuck out our legs to the side and slept.
We sleep still, our bones in pieces, rising finally to light in a gravel pit.
Is that it, little girl? How our lives return to be storied?
You always were a reader. Apart then and now from where you ought
to be, nibbling shoots of spring grass, savoring long days.
You're taken away by reading. Our story bones foretell your present,
our future, like stalks thrown for the *I Ching*.

Fairy Tale Past Bedtime

If I had half her experience I would remember how I got here, the snake
on the road that jutted its chin out my way, a little footbridge arched
over a creek smoothing pebbles into pearly gems.

I would understand the question, the one the small
man asked after we'd made love, the question that I missed, that left me
walking down a soft dirt road alone, fiddleheads unfurling by my side.

Experience and memory aside, right here a flock of ducks spoke spring.
The light at supper pressed its advantage on the night,
kept our juniper's snow birds crackling long past their bed time.

Those other events are insinuating that my life is a story, but the truth
is the tilt of the fierce chin, the pearly pebble,
how small and tender that man was, the forgotten one.

Out of Gas, Star Date Unknown

Tomorrow evening I expect to be in the desert
by the side of the road next to my '53 Ford,
gas can in hand, wondering where to get it filled up.

If I have luck, no one will come to pick me up
and after a long time I will quit waiting.
At dusk I will notice through the sheen of a
desert varnish high how light outlines the fine edges
of dry grass, how black lizards come to lie on red sand
for the day's last warmth, and rattlesnakes stretch across
the road like hopscotch lines.

When coyotes start barking and worrying,
and a string of cows and calves rushes
to their barns in obscure directions,
I'll crawl into the backseat
and hum myself to sleep in harmony
with the silent engine.

I Did Not Visit Green

I went to my office. Green visited me,
but I ignored green. It gathered itself
and leapt from the spider plant near a window.
It called itself in from the lawn outside
but I didn't pay attention.
Green wrapped itself in beads around my wrist
but I hid it under my purple sleeve
and pretended it was a watch.
Green faded away from my capris,
turned almost gray.
It sang and sang from the old rubber plant
and I didn't listen.
It rolled around on my desk,
and spelled itself out on a Crayola and a marker.
It fell to the floor on a slip of paper
but I didn't pick green up.
I picked up my black pen.
I hovered over a white page.

Other Fish to Fry

Fish visited last night, shimmied and swished
in a new clear creek running deep
and fast past our front door.
From the threshold where I stood
I watched minnows grow into fat sunfish
and speckled trout, good eating and beautiful.
Our house filled with people I knew slightly;
political negotiations darted like birds come
down our chimney and trapped among lamps,
windows, and screened back door. I looked away
from the tall people for a moment, got hold
of a single clear notion, bent down.
Children, I said to those at my legs,
You can catch those fish. You can open
the door, step into your boats and go.

Set to Szymborska's Poem "Breughel's Two Monkeys"

I still dream about not finding my classroom only I am the teacher.
If I get there either I or some of my students are naked, a classic.
A fire alarm rings and we run around the room yelling.
Suddenly it is night and red flames glower through the windows.
Ahem, I say, the examination will be on The History of Womankind.
I stammer and hedge trying to find the booklets, the pencils.
The back of the room is edged with men who are taking notes.
My mentor, a famous poet, makes love to a student on a tiny desk.
The other mentor, the other famous poet, crouches on another desk.
It's clear I don't know what to do or if I'm still here.
Did one of them look my way?
Outside the classroom the college burns red in the dark.

Conversations that Do Not Grow Old

He submits to class a story about a boy:
wherever the story boy steps
new flowers pearl up out of the dirt.
He likes to talk at office hours about the nature
of things, big things, miracles, mysteries, magic. I say no,
I don't believe in that. Not even God. Only
this magic:
He is that boy in the story.

I could say   *my thinking skin clothes a mind*   *my breath*
 you here in this office   *my father's death*   *your hand*
finding a beloved book just as I wished   *your toddler, my grown son,*
river long talk   *a poem with white flowers*
          pearl
this cut philodendron rooting in a coffee mug
that Yeats was and is
no difference   that magic from this
strands woven of quantum joy   *silver trout girls*
     running away across a shore

Consider the cherry tree. It is always in bloom.

1.
His body flutters. His thoughts escape
in broken sentences about a boat,
the Mayflower, a journey.
We have been reading the Zen master Dogen
about ever blooming cherry trees.

I look over his crushed legs and back
through the sealed window to an unfamiliar landscape.
A budding cherry tree, vernal equinox, his bones I dream
flowing to Dogen's place where bones are always whole.

2.
Through the sealed windows hills sleep lightly brown,
tomorrow a haze of green.
Clouds sailing in blue lakes move from frame to frame,
tomorrow rain.

His bones work silently,
blasts and plasts speed their business
like many fingers at their needles
darning, mending tattered sails.

The hills sleep lightly brown.
In a moment, haze of green.
Small clouds sail in blue lakes
from frame to frame.
Now rain.

The bones of our son, the blasts and plasts
stitch together silently.
In a moment, he stands.

He stood, he cannot stand, he will stand.
He walked, he cannot walk, he will walk.

3.
I interrupt this meditation because to do otherwise would be to lie. While we are here, the Iraq war breaks out. Our nurse's son is over there, infantry, she is up all night here watching the tv reports while doing the thousand urgent good turns nurses do, agents of that ever blooming healing if healing is to be while we all wonder if her boy will make it back at all. Sometimes is there always peace?

4.
We leave this hospital as if its white were winter
and we slept the nightmares of bears
afraid to wake and find it again   still   winter.
We leave this hospital as if it were snow caves,
home, mercy, tender, eternal, as if we dream
red blood cells seeding in the deep rivers of bone.
Outside the sealed windows and the hissing door

out of the ground push the bent backs of ferns,
out of their pedicels shoot the curled tongues of iris,
and from the brown bumps on branches
explode the cherry blossoms.
We leave this hospital
as if he has always been flowering.

David is Visited by the Gods Before his CABG

David Guerrero, *warrior*, is in the great ball court
near Veracruz. His blood is suckled from his chest
to nourish the ball playing divines, the stars.
The feathered serpent king Quetzalcoatl kneels,
cuts out Guerrero's heart and holds it up—
a beating gift for the gods.
Tomorrow a gloved surgeon in green mask and blue apron
will stop it and chill it and plumb it and warm it
and start it again in the house of his flesh.

The Tyranny of the Sick

is in their trembling request for water or apple juice or more
or less heat or quiet or a brighter lamp,

another music station or another movie or another, or a pillow
under the head, the hip, the foot, the arms, just so;

(picture Captain Kirk of Starfleet Command)

is in the clammy white forehead, untrimmed beard, the forgetfulness
of repetitive minutes and hours in which the sick person is captive

to escapades of blood pressures, embarrassments of vomit, halos
    of pain relief
detailed notations of blood, vomit and pain relief;

is in their belief or hope that love resides in you as bountiful as a well,
and is in the truth that yes, you pour your love as freely as mountain rain.

The gift of the sick is their laughter.
The sick person says he is happy to help you attain enlightenment.

Sometime in Late August We Return Home

Someone asks us if we've had any summer at all.   We eat fresh corn and green beans and both taste like afternoon rain. A hummingbird buzzes by.

Once the cat stayed out late celebrating the scurrying dark warm.

A hospital room is seasonless, or name the season Disinfectant, or Many Sheet Changes, or Season of Hard Light, Season of Steel Taste.

Summer is found there in what others bring, a yellow peach and a book titled Levity.

Gray moth wings spill out of the patient nurses' pockets, some pockets are stuffed with sparrows' beaks.

Our daughter had a day of summer drowsing on a couch near an open window, a fan blurring time. Because it was summer, she rose only to kiss her lover good-bye, again and again.

We went home for a day and summer fell red from the cherry tree into our jars filled with sugar. The uncut lawn wild as a meadow promised more summer to come.

When soft rain came we wore it in our hair and carried it back to the hospital where through a window summer lightning broke and broke horizon to horizon, broke trees and rocks, and the wind leaned so hard on trees they broke, but not the window.

By late summer, battalions of black flies woke to feed on the dead and living, and our horse woke in the hot afternoon to escape the flies, to kick up dust, to lie and roll in the dust.

The dry wind kicked up dust, we tasted it.

The migrant hummingbird now hovers before our cat, her white throat a lily. The cat's eyes go even bigger and rounder with surprise, and the dog laughs as the bird helicopters up and away.

Caretaker of Broken Various and the Saints

A burden, yes, though when you try on "a blessing" instead
      (as if everything's value is dressed in how you name it)
then a few saints circle your peripheral vision. Not a believer,
you're unsure of who the saint of caretakers is, or are, though, oh yes,
you know there are plenty of sainted caretakers, take *St. Julian l'Hospitalier*
in Flaubert, he holds the sickening body, the body shedding gobs of skin,
          oozing all matter of matter, yellowed, blackened, parched,
          and finally Julian sleeps holding this wretched flesh, this man,
          against his own healthy body,
          and the fellow turns out to be Jesus.
There's the one from the black and white movie about Lourdes, the girl
 who kept seeing Mary, was it Mary? smiling there, the girl dragging her useless
legs to the French waters; but she is neither caretaker nor protector
of caretakers, she's the "taken care of"
so you return to your filing system of your potential patron saints,
and there is the Virgin from the movie, now in color,
her starry blue cape, her golden moon-crowned wimple.
She gazes down at you with such pity, you beloved blessed caretaker you.
For the caretaker needs caretaking, a truth preached over
and over because it's a secret.

There's the Pope. Not the Pope.

Then you catch sight of the saint who wears a brown broad-brimmed hat
loaded with bird seed. That's the trick. He walks with his hands out, palms up,
cupping the air swirling with snowy plover, meadowlarks, western blue-birds
and red-wing blackbirds. St. Francis.
Instead of remaining in the caretaker's room
you want to walk with him this morning in just such a hat brimming with seed
into a pasture touched with first snow, walk with his arm around your shoulder,
your own hands open, cupped with oats. They'll come, the furry horses,
licking and chewing, like friendly dragons, their breath steaming.

HORSE SAYS

I Hold my Childhood Novels Responsible and My Parents' Cowboy Ballads, Too

Black Beauty, My Friend Flicka, Man O'War, Misty of Chincoteague

When I go into the meadow I ask him about his day. I run my hands over his skin to read his answers, feeling for bites and bumps, gashes and burrs, his accounts of rolls in the dust or mud, about the pigeons and egrets who rode on his back and didn't care where they shat. I hold his hooves briefly to read their temperature. I try to read the story in his deep brown eyes, whether he had enough to eat, whether the mare next field paid him any mind, whether he spent any time today thinking about when he was caught and taken from his herd. I read the direction of his ears—is he happy to see me—and the purple flowers in his mane, look for the story of the pasture's season. As the sun sets and I get ready to leave, I decide to try again to learn more of his past life, and ask him to tell me about how, when he was caught, he was already a grown stallion with a harem. When I ask him about his history, I know from his bill of sale, his brand, his scars, that he's a mustang, hard broke, with a story of tight ropes and heavy packs. He knickers, blows, huffs, flinches, squeals, neighs, but more of his story I'll never know. If only he could write a memoir, *My Life as a Gelding*; a play, *No Way Out*; a novel of romance and rescue, *The Great Utah and Colorado Caper*; if only he could record some cowboy ballads. He loves to hear me sing *Red River Valley* and *Home, Home on the Range*.

A Glove of Frost, a Finger of Ice, November

Seven rock doves skate in their tiny shoes
across our driveway.
My hair tastes like blowing snow.
My nose breathes leaf mold.
My ears are broken ukuleles.
I see a white feather on that red stone.
Children of Eve, of Lucifer, of John,
the rock doves petrify on branches
wrapped neck to neck
in their one black scarf.

There are no scarves, only acrid car exhaust
and Mr. Vulture cracking a puddle.
The new president could be the wind,
the slick floor of midnight.

Sophia's Dream of the Horse

Everything seems difficult. She has a dream one night of riding her horse, her real horse in a dreamscape that is like the memory: grassy meadow, ditches running so full the frogs are singing, and white clover on the ground and snow in the sky at the same time. The important thing is that the wild horse has chosen to love her without any fear, has chosen to let her lie along his broad back with her arms wrapped around his tossing neck while he runs, her fingers laced in his black coarse mane, and he has chosen to let her tell him where to go with only the slightest changes in breath and weight. See how it is? He is wild and strong-headed, he's been harmed by people before, he is difficult, we could say this is a dream about nature, he wants to let her lead, to let her go with him wherever she wants, and what she wants is what he wants. It can be like this sometimes, even when you're nearly a child still and every measure of your day or the nation or the planet screams disaster.

You despair reading the news, knowing an oil spill the size of Alaska will reach long southern shores and wrap each grain of white sand, shroud every feather, every flower's wing in black. You imagine miniscule stained-glass windows, the shining diatoms, dimming, and the eyes of fishes going flat, their gills and the fairy legs of shrimp tethered by black strings, and the bowed necks of tarry gannets. The dream does not say different. It can't heal the sea, the shore. In the dream, the white-dotted meadow is beautiful drinking snow, it goes on forever, and she is riding a wild being and her own wildness answers the horse's and he answers her love.

Grieving the Yaks

They startled, leaping, black skirts
swirled and draped ankle length,
ribboning pelts revealed
pointed feet impossibly petite.
They used gravity backwards,
and propelled skyward
above their frozen field,
twisting at the apex of an arc
to ward off their pasture mates,
earth bound buffaloes
and pushy horses shouldering for oats.

All the four-leggeds are dancers of merit,
but the yaks are the Martha Graham dancers
dressed in sweeping full black gowns,
gigantic masked heads and dark kohl eyes,
antlers expressing in late modernist glyphs
primordial states of rage or fear or hunger.

The mental state of yaks
is Gloria Swanson on the staircase
in Sunset Boulevard, back of hand against her forehead.
The yaks do not mar the screen with speech:
silent in their queries, unreachable in their gaze,
hanging back when the food bucket appeared
(the buffalos acting as stage crew,
and Doc the alpha horse arriving to direct)
still their toeing of the dirt mimed a desire
that felled me. I should have written
this when I first met them. So let me say exactly this:

When they danced, and dance they did
until they lay down upon the land
and died, the pasture was their stage.

As a Newt, I Found Summer to be Disastrous

The condition of my skin determines the condition of my health.
When my colony and I perceived the margin of our pond
drawing an ever-smaller circle on its clay beach
we decided to crawl out to seek bigger waters
and failing that, have a worthy adventure before desiccation.

It is in my nature to hang stilly in warm still shallows of a silty pond,
to meditate on the nature and meaning of immortality,
to brush shoulders with other newts,
to draw in insects and algae with a slight slow
opening and shutting of my mouth,
to sift oxygen from water with the slowest fanning
of my external lungs.

Instead, I stepped out, tiptoed for many days and nights
across wire sharp sand and ticking grass
trying to keep my tender belly clear. My palms calloused.
I sheltered from sun beneath the shadows of stones,
singing whenever I could a song for rain.
I thus arrived at your door to ask for a dish of water
before tip-toing on across your asphalt drive.

This Horse, Too

Twilight bounds softly over the grass. James Wright

The deep red brown of this mustang
pulls sadness in a long hot thread from my chest.
He steps sideways, careful, to my hand.
I lean my forehead into his neck and breathe.
He crushes oats and purple flowers into sweet exhales.
Thin white scars ribbon his belly, neck, and back
from the ropes of his breaking.
He grew up wild, his past silenced into gazing at sunset,
into studying ibis' and cranes' silhouettes
migrating above gates and fences,
into listening with a horse's yearning attention
to mournful desert ballads I sing into his soft ears.
He is perfect in his dark-eyed kindness.
There is no loneliness like his.
He pulls the thread of sadness and I follow him
into the shadowed river of his lost canyons.

The Paint Horse Founders

She wakes me as if she were a baby in the next room,
as if I needed to hear if she were breathing,
listen for the whimper of hunger.
She shifts from foot to foot in her dirt floor stall,
her own smooth tonnage hurting her.
She thinks about lying down to rest her split feet,
understands she'd be hard pressed to get up ever.
She knows in the pasture outside her fence
moonlight shines on thick spring leaves
that were lush enough to lame her.
Her desire is limitless.

Chained Dog Dreams: Open Window

Does the chained dog try to break her chain, her collar,
test which breaks first, her windpipe or the steel?
Or does the chained dog wait,
barking hunger for chow kibble,
her thirst for clean water,
her longing for the person to return?
Is the chained dog saying in the short sharp yaps,
"I'm here   I'm here   I'm here?"
If she knew how, the chained dog would write a novel,
proving that her poetic freedom can never be chained,
describing life on a farm with puddles to lap,
pole fences to skinny under, gophers to dig for;
beyond the farm a rabbity fragrant forest.
The story breaks her heart when the facts show through.

To Pray at the Altar of this Horse

you must prophecy good weather, for whether blizzard
or sand wind or sun you must find him far out in a field
and when you approach him you must look down aside.
You must ring the bells of the halter buckles,
square your shoulders and stand strong
or back away slowly facing him,
head up, eyes down, as if for a king.
You must joke around about heelers and gophers.
You must scratch his withers
before you bend your neck
and push your head into his shoulder
for he might turn away.
You must brush off the mud on his coat
with curry comb and bristles
for he rolls in puddles and ditches.
You must pick gorse out of his tail with apologies
for he prefers to sleep tangled in the bush when it's cold.
You must accept his hooves into your hands to pick them.
You must clean his sheath and foreskin respectfully.
You must never get under his feet without his knowing.
You must teach yourself to be a handmaid
who wipes his eyes, strips gnats from his ear-linings,
massages his scars, and checks his teeth.
When you pray at his shoulder,
you must accept the odors of mouth and tail,
must adore the smell of his skin.
When you pray, you must breathe hair and dust
into your mouth and be grateful.
Once he is prepared, you must give him an offering:
oats or graham crackers or alfalfa hay.
As the sun drops low and the first star shows,
you must humble yourself, so if he says
I'm ancient, so home, home is where we need to go,
you must not doubt him.

Horse Says

One: I'm not the source of this love that sparks
soft fireworks between your fingers and my coat. Love spills
out of your fingertips brushing mosquitoes, pulling gorse,
and scratching, scratching my hide. Love is in the lover, not so
much the beloved. I love equally my oats, meadow
grass, wet mud on hot days, the mare in the next field, and you
brushing out my winter coat until my wild stripes show.

Two: I'm in the pasture and oats will arrive one day when
you're through moving things, moving objects here and
there, your daughter out of the house, your son back
to his plane with his luggage, yourselves in
all four directions, cars breaking, bolts and oil raining, carbon
shooting out your car's exhaust as you shuttle objects back and forth between
stores and dorm rooms, stores and your homes, meals onto and off tables,
candles got out and lit and burned and snuffed, all the while,
I'm waiting in the deep grass, eating, and one day you'll arrive
and you'll be carrying my oats.

Three: Take this with you, this you cantering bareback, this you
I carry across the last green meadow of fall, take yourself
this way, and this meadow, and me, into every closed room,
take this outdoor you, carry yourself as I carry you, broadly, strong, indoors
and as I try to swerve out from under you, take yourself laughing,
hanging on as I jostle into a trot, take the one who threads her fingers
through my coarse mane, take the laughing one, almost falling off,
always holding on, crossing autumn's meadows, take this
you laughing into the rooms of winter.

My Galapagos

Wild, not wary   a blue booby teeters
      checks its foot, preens its shoulder

to shoulder with a satisfied pelican   craw a possible grin

to shoulder with a tortoise
her shell an acre vast   her stroll
      paddling tiptoe

these creatures all equally assured
the observer's gaze benign.   And in their eyes a squall

of penguins   a green slow
wave, black pumice, a curving hip of sand beach. Incredible. I

have not been there but when you waltz four-footed   crooked white blaze
over our salty dry meadow   even hungry your gentle glance aside

I believe.   In my calm hands nothing
      but open.

Horse   God   Bird   Congregation

Once you look down at his
hooves dangerously
close to your bare toes and think
he is a god, this horse, meaning
in him is the spark that sparks you, meaning
you hold him in awe, meaning
the spring wind blows hard because
of his presence in the field, meaning
he is present in the field because
of the strong spring wind (as in
butterfly effect as in
causation without comprehension as in
intention without consequence or
with consequence)
once you do this
something (innate metaphor-makers that we are)
compels you to continue, so that
when you lean and stumble alongside
his dusty warm side you are
leaning and stumbling with god
and in this syllogism
leaning, stumbling, side, wind, become
weighted with it, with resonance, referents,
resinous, enough to make
your chest contract
and if you say, *look,*
the horse is sleeping
you are saying *god is sleeping*
and the horse asleep becomes
a kind of waking, awakening,
listening to the wind as
it splits around his ears, becomes
a waiting, for on the wind blows
grass, blows falling water, blow
coyote and cougar. Sleeping becomes
the un-resting awareness of a horse
the awareness of god.

Being still in the wind and leaning become
shared context, shared awareness, then
affection, and you are
the part of the divine
he calls to, as you
called to him, and then the credo
god is love
means something, something
alive and true and specific, incarnate;
you understand how
loving a thing can make
you god.
In the morning
you look out your window
to the east you see him
the horse chocolate against
perfectly blue clear sky
chocolate against bright spring green grass *(see)*
you see him grazing in the wind
beautiful and startling and more startling when a
congregation of yellow-headed
blackbirds flies down and gathers at his feet
(see chocolate, green, blue, black, breeze, yellow splashed)
gargling and buzzing harshly the way
yellow-headed blackbirds do
first in May. They peck and sip along
with him as he moves, the wind
ruffling their bent heads and swaying
his sweeping black tail, *(splashing)* all is
springtime bird racket
water drip, ooze and
motion and now
it is easy to think
congregation, easy to think
choir, easy to laugh at
us clustered at the feet
of god who graciously ignores

us, busy as we are
in the midst of plenty and later when
he moves smoothly (he walks
as if slightly above earth, elevated over green by
wings invisible, or as if rocking over sea—some
element less earth) right over
to the alkaline dirt where he throws
himself down, kicks his big feet in the air,
rolls and rolls, rises in clown face, ghost sheet.

WOMAN DESCENDING A STAIR

Look at Us Becoming Older with Grace

We are waiting for a visit from someone else's children. I made spaghetti sauce and think about baking cookies.

I pulled several favorite picture books to read to the children.

He's napping, and the twenty year old cat is napping on him. I have cut out book reviews to save in my journal so I can remember to read the books that interest me. One is about loss. Another is about a cat who goes bed to bed in a nursing home, spending the night with whoever is next to die. Another one is by a mortician poet, celebrating death. I haven't even noticed the similarity of themes.

The house is full of quiet and is mostly clean. I listen to myself thinking. I am aware of general happiness and calm as clear and light as desert air. It wasn't like this once. Someone else's children will believe we always lived in peace.

Portal of Cries

Do you remember how you cried as a baby,
no thoughts, a tunnel full of grief
overflowing out your mouth,
a geyser of scream?
I hear someone next door
crying this way, the pitch clearly a baby's.
An offshore drilling rig in the Gulf
is this baby's throat, the black spill
unstoppable as her grief,
tarring the oceans, blacking the starry
disks of diatoms and mouths of coral.

Although you arrived
silent, saved the cries for later,
perhaps for the first blood
drawn from your tiny round foot,
many arrive with the scream ready to spill
at the burn of their first intake
of air. I fancied I might give you
a baby-cry-less life—
inevitably you woke up someplace
and didn't know where you were and
cried with the grief and fright natural
to a kidnapped galactic traveler,
a gypsy, an orphan, someone
piping grief from another universe.

I have heard gravity
must come from elsewhere like
babies do, since we have too little
to account for its strength.
It leaks like a diaper
from a gravity rich
universe, rising through
sidewalk cracks
and under the doors
at basement stairs. It must

rain on us, too, sticky particles
from window sills landing on our brains
or solar plexuses as we lie on
the ground at night.
Dispersed, we are used to it.
Our tiny baby push-ups
and our first steps defy it.
But when the baby cries she pipes it pure.
We hear her and walk down her street
with our heads bent, shoulders
stooped. We hardly lift our boots.

Birth Epic (Abridged)

The birthing a success by its most important measure:
        the baby alive.

The father and friends toasting with champagne in recovery
over the limp but smiling, stitched up mother,
the pediatrician arrives by skis
        a blizzard still spinning outside.

        the baby alive   if awfully overgrown
with long nails, peeling skin, and lungs full of meconium
kept in intensive care on oxygen   wired to antibiotics
pricked half-hourly in the foot to measure blood oxygen levels

        I could hear the baby scream and could not touch.

Do you know the literature of birth stories?
An oral literature, added to by new mothers everywhere,
each mother's tale repeated, epic ingredients perfected:
        Through will-less heroism and the caprice of gods
        she gives to her people a gift from the other world.
what went well, what right. The terrible mistakes.
        Always a measure of terror.

Call it *post-partum anxiety post-partum depression* call it
        post-traumatic stress syndrome
like soldiers get. Mother has crossed the border between death and life.
No books, no manual, no survivors' groups for when the baby lives.
        If everything goes well the idea is
the baby makes you forget. The urgency of its need,
        its cries silence yours before they flower.
Sleeping sweet, chuckling, the baby in your arms
        has power to comfort you.
The O of its waking. The rose of its yawn. The yoga of its breath.
        The godhead of its living. Euphoria ecstasy
orgasmic nirvana of its tiny sucking, feeding.

        Give a veteran of the trenches his healthy baby.

Look at the women sitting together telling their war stories.

It was a success by any measure, my baby alive.
        What if it were calling from down the hall
and I couldn't hold it? Later, gowned green in the white room
I rocked alone and touched baby fingers. I have read the fingers
        astonish most, little alien with thumbs, miniature
        lined knuckles   perfectly like ours.

The tale:
Through a blizzard we drove across town, across railroad tracks
        to the birth center. Every bounce a quiet agony.
My (mostly) faithful husband at the helm. He had done with
        refinishing the changing table.
Together we entered the antechamber of birth, the
        politically correct cozy affirming quilted homelike midwives' island.
They heard what we had to say,
        timed the contractions, measured dilation (peering in, ahem),
said, "You're not ready."
I breathed Lamaze meditation. Appeared beatific.

We ferried back and forth for three days.
The gates to the otherworld remained sealed despite the flood
(concealed as a broken pickle jar in the supermarket).
My cervix opened enough for a pomegranate seed
        but not a baby's head.
        Why not?

        Over-ready baby trapped above my cervix,
        too big for my bones, my pubic bones dividing,
                the slow deep ache of cartilage and bone splitting.

(I feel those bones again lately. An indulgence to say so. What could it
matter now? My baby old enough to vote.)

The baby and I were eventually saved
(note passive construction)

when a green suited surgeon flew in, furious
at the midwives mistaking
my condition. Furious,
the baby inside drowning, dying.
The surgeon cursed and ordered people around,
shot me up, cut
that baby out. Saved our lives.
I kiss his hem, I kiss his ring.

I think he hated me.
                    Smelled something.

I felt I was a repulsive, bloody failure.
            But whose epic is this anyway?
And who faces survivor duty: to make meaning of events, to decide
            if they are accidental, purposeful, contextual.
Decide to forgive. Whom to forgive and whom to hold
                    accountable.
Whom to teach what to do next time.
Know what midwives failed to know.
Mother and author and hero.

We could use this were we misogynists.
All us women screwing up, inept, the women's center failing.
But I must use it. What a reach,
            feminist politics stirred into our little drama
except that's always the way with private difficulties.

            Especially birth. War. The battlefield is a white hall
            click click click of shoes on hard floors
            or rice fields where quiet women squat
            unintentionally, caught off guard as if in a taxi,
            or the heaped pyres where women were burned
            for practicing midwifery.
            What was destroyed must be rediscovered.

And when did midwifery begin? When we first walked erect.
From the time we were human, we needed help.
That squatting thing? Urgency, not choice.
The genesis story of pain begins when baby brains grew big
when women began carrying in their wombs
the potential to know what gods know.

I would have liked to know what is known about hormones now:
our urge to be with others is from
"rational anxiety, as human as our opposable thumbs."[1]
I might have told the midwives, "Please drop by.
I've just mopped the floor."

And when in our country did the first woman attend college?
Who is the first woman doctor? When? When did a woman become an
obstetrician?
When were midwives kept from obstetrical knowledge? From the dark ages on,
with the advent of the patriarchal religion Christianity.
When were midwifes allowed to know what obstetricians know?
When did the guild of midwives start again?

Study the testimony of Margaret Sanger, nurse mid-wife who became a pioneer
for contraception, for choice.

After what we've been through, I'm for all the knowledge there is—pagan,
underground, intuitive, folk, female, male, matriarchal, patriarchal,
hierarchical, western, eastern, scientific, mechanistic, intuitive, warm, cold,
homely, institutional—to be there for every
       birthing woman, as needed.

---

[1] Angier, Natalie. *Woman.* Page 309

II.

The second time, I picked my birth assistant
from the testimony of other women.
Oh, and the first guy, when I showed up,
said, "You know you're really old to do this"
and lost my business.
My choice, the reverend Dr. Hardee,
said I wasn't. But I was.
This baby conceived from an old egg
in an old womb developed placenta in the wrong place (previa)
so the odds were fifty fifty, he said eventually,
on the baby and my surviving.
The epic journey focused on keeping still,
traveling only to nearby medical facilities.

These were the tasks, the hero's tests:
Give a quart of fresh blood weekly
just in case I'd need it;
have my fluid levels checked daily
—there wasn't enough,
(the car metaphor is unavoidable)
and the baby couldn't float;
lie on my left side 20 hours a day
to feed better the baby's heart;
feel for the baby's fluttering movements,
count and record them;
monitor constantly its heart
for skipping, missing, rapid beats.

I grew fat with listening,
silent with listening,
jaw-clenched with listening,
strong.

I saw into the otherworld
through veil and water,

through dream and sonogram:
a photo of its every chromosome
and on the video screen
its snub-nosed profile,
its sucking mouth, its thumb,
its vulva a miniature orchid.

Still it came to the sort of crisis
one cannot be prepared for:
blood gushing as from a warrior's chest
when stabbed through by sword
he staggers, presses his hands against his heart,
and cannot stop the flow;
fear so fierce my knees
flopped violently, as when from pounding chariots
and horses weighted down with mail
the earth quakes at 9.5 on the Richter scale.

Then the baby's heart echoing from the otherworld
became silent on the monitor,
silent as a smoking battlefield
the living have left to spoil.

Around my naked body,
spread out on the gurney
and still as a corpse
(I barely nodded yes, yes, yes to everything, anything)
the medical team, those demigods,
rushed, shaving and injecting.
As I went under (no time for niceties,
the mother alert in the birth room)
I heard them say, don't let this woman
ever get pregnant again.
This woman? Was that I?

Post-traumatic stress?
Ask the day nurse about the time I buzzed her

and sobbing said my baby's eyes were sewn
forever shut with black silky threads
as soft as lashes.
The attendants in the preemie ward
laughed about it for a week.
Once home I wouldn't sleep, on vigil to her breath.
I woke her just to see her eyes
flip open like a doll's.

The Babylonian King Gilgamesh's friend
Enkidu died; he could not save him.
He lost the herb that gives immortality.
We could say that first hero's journey was a failure
except he learned to live and write his story.

   The baby had the power to comfort
by the O of its waking. The rose of its yawn. The yoga of its breath.
  The godhead of its living. Euphoria ecstasy

orgasmic nirvana of its tiny sucking, feeding.

  What poor warrior has that.

Woman Descending a Stair

This morning I reveal myself to be an onion,
           —layered body not psyche
            poignant and pungent—
comfortable as a week old bruise,
my own familiar Walla Walla, my sweet hot Bermuda.
The slip of a scallion I used to be—
                its sweet green stretches within.

Or my stomach, a sheet on a clothesline
                hangs between the two clothespins of my hips
    bulging in a warm breeze.
Once it blew slightly in toward the house of my bones.

My body's delicate beauty by way of love and childbirth
became this risen brown loaf.
        I thank it for the yeasty promise it held,
        how it withstood the punch down,
        the kneading, the heat,
        and provided.

I had thought my girl all gone.
She dances under the skin of my skin,
a whole frog kicking inside a snake's stretched gut.

She's an undertow tugging below a calm sea.

Old Marrieds' Song in September

When I was single and not promised
married and unmarried came to my bed,
their vows I considered their business
justice not mine to decide,

but since I have promised you only
even a dream full of lust
is repressed at the first kiss of longing
as my conscience whispers our trothe.

The man with the clean shaven cheek
makes my skin heat like before,
but you stand quiet in the shadow
neither glance nor smile to reprove.

Dance with me on the rough boards of the deck.
The moon is a quarter or so.
The coyote is wooing our dogs with her song
and we won't be sleeping tonight.

Apology Begins with If I could

you know   turn
the house into cake   brown bread

sparrow crumbs, birthday siftings, spackle into
windows into mouse lenses   I would let it

crumble around you with the children playing together
building up block towns under summer sky

pumpkins their slick guts
spread
indoor snowman: in all this

no reasons left for you to cry. See
the tulips profuse and flailing in the beauty of green yard.

The sun would never again prepare to set.

You would play on clean carpet beach together
the live long sunshiny day.

I would be quiet and happy.

Sex, Birth, and Death

I remember when I discovered sex, an unexplained country, mine
to colonize and rule. I lived there till it became more like
a green island resort to visit when I could afford to.

I became the first pregnant woman in the world,
first visitor to another planet orbiting a near star where I arrived
glorious, proud, alone, posting my flag and singing my song
till I had to leave it, hastily, for another universe: childbirth and motherhood.

And now, who am I? Not the child who sees fairies entering doors
at the roots of trees, who talks to a minute oarsman
paddling a small water strider over a snow melt puddle.

No. I come alone to the milky way of death, find its galaxy lurking
like a dime in a scarf drawer, or leaping, a cricket, out of a pot of lavender,
or pouring out, dark honey, from the pages of shelved books.

Or I step onto its shore and turn my foot slowly in its sand,
then step back, of course afraid. This last country,
and the fear of it, like everything before, mine alone,
my invention, one that I wind up in the morning so it uncoils and hums
through the day here, under my rib-cage,
animating me with its metallic whir.

The Land of the Indeterminately Aged

I am not waiting for any lost pets to wander back,
they are finally, certainly long dead by now.
It is today I am forgetting, the press of my lips
on my daughter's warm forehead, on my own sleeve,
on the glass window in our door, cold.
What can I distinguish now
of *mother, father,* names that are not names?
Laura, I say now, for mother,
and Michael, for father, we have arrived
at the land of the indeterminately aged,
where *mother father* and *child*
boil and rise, boil and turn like alphabet pasta in soup
and I wash your hands, you dry my face,
we sit at a round table and take turns serving.

Time to See

If you live through it long enough
                    maybe fifty, sixty years
and you drive on a narrow paved road you remember
from when it was a dirt rut between Gardner and Redwing

and you look back on your lovers
                                        even the abuser
and if you can love who you have become
                        sagging knees, bunion, and all, you see
        how they each tried for love in their own ways,
and you thank them in your breath
                with your mouth's tongue curled around dark coffee, generous
                        with bitter. This is peace.

Like Siddhartha, your face that you love as well as any face,
            just a lined old face,
gathered their sorrows and hope in feathered lines over your bones.

Your friends and sisters
            even the ones you've quit sending cards to
                        (unless you count tomorrow's sympathy card
                        something about great trees falling and acorns)
            those for whom the news clipping of a beloved painter's elegy curls
                to silence in a closed drawer of things meant to be shared,
each friend in her way smoothes your freckled hand,
cups your chin softly in her absent hand
            as surely as your partner sits in the seat next to you.

If you live, say, past fifty,
        though you could decide to see
this now or
yesterday,
you look in the rearview mirror
of your dusty station wagon and you see
all the way back to peace, which is willows
                bending along the roadside
                        red in winter, gold in spring, white

with catkins, green, then gold, then
red again, and an irrigation ditch rushing full in the spring at their roots,

or to peace out the passenger window, which is surely
a foal teething on her first pale shoots of grass
and you look ahead to peace, which is an umbrella shaded picnic table
in a small yard where a father you've not met
back home alive from whatever war it was this time
rests and cradles his swaddled baby,

and down this road to peace on the horizon where the moon and sun
hang together in one deep sky

and you see your life was always meant to drive this road.

THANKS

While I am grateful to too many to list here who have welcomed these poems or figured in them, I must particularly thank Gail Coray, my sister and ideal reader, who gave a generous and critical reading of each poem with open heart and meticulous care over many hours of phone calls. Thanks to Annie Dawid, Pam Noble, my children Galen and Sophia, and of course David, who received them with such strong emotions and clear understanding I knew I had something worth sharing more broadly. Thanks to Cynda for offering me quiet workspace in her Peace Cottage. I also thank the many people who contributed to providing me a few days of retreat at the Crestone Mountain Zen Center in the middle of a year with a heavy work load; in those wide open days, I heard again my poet self and saw the book that could be.

Carol D. Guerrero-Murphy works as a writer, teacher, and editor from her home in Superior, Colorado. She lives with her husband, photographer David Diaz Guerrero, and two cats. She is the WILLA Award Finalist author of *Table Walking at Nighthawk* (Ghost Road Press 2007) and has published widely in journals and anthologies. She has a doctorate in English/Creative Writing from Denver University and is now a professor emerita, teaching part time in the College Prison Program of Adams State University. The setting for many of these poems is the San Luis and Huerfano Valleys in Southern Colorado where she lived for many years and in Alaska where she grew up. This is her second full length book of poetry.

CPSIA information can be obtained
at www.ICGtesting.com
Printed in the USA
FFHW021443081119
56015362-61901FF